GREGORY L. VOGT

MARS

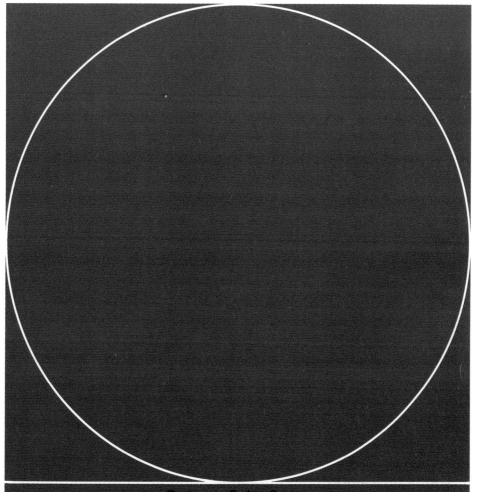

Gateway Solar System
The Millbrook Press
Brookfield, Connecticut

Published by The Millbrook Press
2 Old New Milford Road
Brookfield, Connecticut 06804

Library of Congress Cataloging-in-Publication Data
Vogt, Gregory.
Mars / Gregory L. Vogt.
p.   cm.
Includes bibliographical references and index.
Summary: Presents information on Mars, the reddish-orange planet,
and its exploration by the U.S. spacecraft *Mariner* and *Viking*.
Includes a glossary and "Mars Quick Facts."
ISBN 1-56294-392-8 (lib. bdg.)
1. Mars (Planet)—Juvenile literature.   2. Project Mariner—
Juvenile literature.   3. Viking Mars Program—Juvenile literature.
[1. Mars (Planet).   2. Space flight to Mars.   3. Project Mariner.
4. Viking Mars Program.]   I. Title.   II. Series: Vogt, Gregory.
Gateway solar system.
QB641.V6   1994
523.4'3—dc20   93-11219 CIP   AC

Photographs and illustrations courtesy of
National Aeronautics and Space Administration, except
U.S. Geological Survey, Flagstaff, Arizona: pp. 4, 20, 21;
Jet Propulsion Laboratory: pp. 15, 16, 17, 23.

Solar system diagram by Anne Canevari Green

MARS

This picture of Mars was pieced together from about one hundred separate photographs taken by the *Viking* spacecraft.

Once every 780 or so Earth days, Earth and the planet Mars are on exactly the same side of the sun. This sometimes brings the two planets as close as 35 million miles (56 million kilometers) to each other. For *astronomers* (scientists who study objects in outer space) that's good news. Seen through their telescopes, Mars seems much larger, and the view of its reddish surface much clearer, than when the planet is farther away.

In 1877 one astronomer took advantage of the closeness of Mars to make some startling drawings of the planet. Giovanni Schiaparelli, working at the Brera Observatory in Italy, made careful sketches of what he saw. Even on very clear nights, the view of the surface of Mars danced and wavered in his telescope. That's because air currents in Earth's atmosphere cause light passing through it to shimmer. Where other astronomers saw shadowy dark areas on the planet, Schiaparelli saw interconnecting lines. He called his dark lines *canali,* an Italian word meaning channels.

In time, other astronomers learned of Schiaparelli's sketches, and some of those astronomers began to see lines on Mars as well. What could the lines be? With each new observation, the lines became sharper in detail and greater in number. Newspaper reporters learned of the discovery. One of them incorrectly translated the word *canali* into the English word "canals." That mistake set off a scientific controversy that was to last nearly a hundred years.

Canals on Earth are built by human beings. If there were canals on Mars, then there must be intelligent life on Mars! Many people, including some astronomers, began to believe that Mars was drying up. They thought that Martians were building canals to move meltwater from the planet's polar ice caps to the drier areas. But not all astronomers believed this. Some, no matter how hard they looked, could see only shadows. When those same astronomers used bigger telescopes to look at Mars, there was no hint of the canals at all. It seemed that the canals were visible only to some astronomers using medium-power telescopes. Perhaps the canals were imaginary.

Ninety-five years after Schiaparelli first saw his *canali,* a spacecraft arrived at Mars. The spacecraft, *Mariner 9,* was launched by the National Aeronautics and Space Administration (NASA). It arrived at Mars and went into

An artist's view of what NASA's *Mariner 9* spacecraft looked like as it approached Mars. The yellow ring shows the spacecraft's orbit. The white rings show the orbits of the planet's two moons.

orbit around the planet. For many months, it took pictures of Mars, and it eventually solved the mystery of the canals.

The Fourth Planet

Mars is the farthest of the rocky planets that orbit the sun. The others are Mercury, Venus, and Earth. Beyond Mars are the *asteroids* (chunks of rock); the giant gas planets Jupiter, Saturn, Uranus, and Neptune; and the ice planet, Pluto.

Mars orbits the sun once every 687 days, at an average distance of 142 million miles (228 million kilometers) from the sun. But Mars's orbit is not very circular, so at times it is closer to the sun and at times farther away. The distance between the closest and farthest points from the sun is about 26 million miles (42 million kilometers).

Being farther from the sun than Earth is means that Mars gets less sunlight than does Earth. As a result, Mars is colder. Its temperature ranges from a high of 71 degrees Fahrenheit (22 degrees Celsius) near its *equator* in the Martian summer to a frigid 193 degrees below zero Fahrenheit (−125 degrees Celsius) at the Martian south pole during winter.

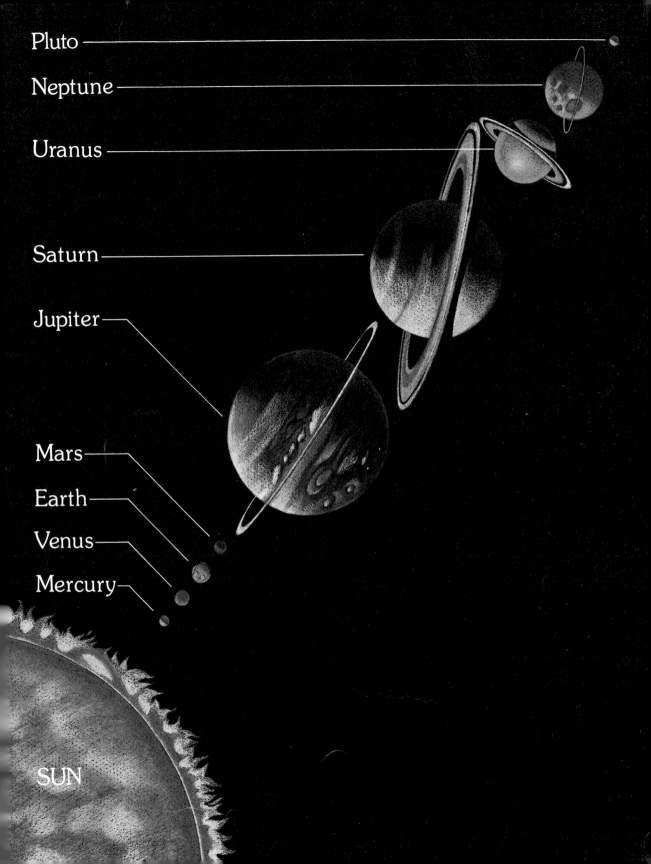

Pluto

Neptune

Uranus

Saturn

Jupiter

Mars

Earth

Venus

Mercury

SUN

Mars is a smaller planet than Earth. Its diameter is 4,222 miles (6,800 kilometers), which makes it about one half the size of Earth. Because it is smaller and less massive, its surface *gravity* (a force that causes objects to attract each other) is smaller, too. If you weigh 100 pounds (45 kilograms) on Earth, you would only weigh 38 pounds (17 kilograms) on Mars!

Partly because of its low gravity, Mars doesn't have much of an atmosphere. Earth's gravity keeps its atmosphere wrapped around the planet like a blanket of gas. But on Mars, most of the gas that may have surrounded the planet when it first formed has escaped into space. The air on Mars is very thin—it has only about one one-hundredth the density of air on Earth. If you were an astronaut exploring the surface of Mars, you would have to wear a space suit. The air on Mars is mostly carbon dioxide gas (the gas you expel when you breathe). There are also very small amounts of other gases, such as nitrogen, oxygen, and water vapor.

Mars is sometimes called the Red Planet because, when seen through a telescope, it has a reddish-orange color. The color comes from rocks and soil that are rich in the chemical iron oxide. This is the material that forms rust on Earth. Since nearly all of Mars is covered with "rusty" rocks and soil, the planet looks reddish orange.

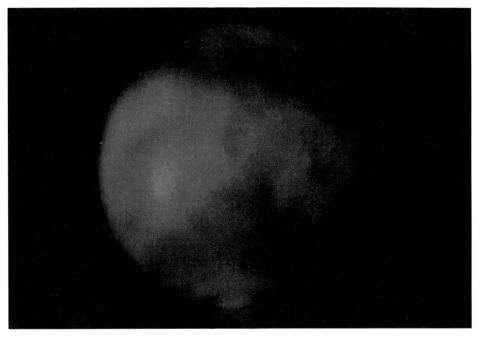

Seen through a powerful telescope on Earth, Mars looks blurry. But the planet's red color shows clearly.

Mars, like Earth, has polar ice caps. The ice caps, which get larger in the Martian winter and smaller in the Martian summer, are bright white. The ice in the polar caps is probably made up of a combination of frozen carbon dioxide gas (dry ice) and water ice.

Two very small, potato-shaped, crater-pocked moons circle Mars. Phobos, the closest to Mars, is about 16 miles (26 kilometers) at its greatest diameter. Deimos, more than twice as far away, is only 9.3 miles (15 kilometers)

The moon Phobos looks like a flying potato orbiting Mars in this picture, taken by a Soviet spacecraft in 1989.

at its greatest diameter. Both moons are believed to be asteroids that passed near Mars and were captured by its gravity.

Mariner 9 *and the Martian Canals*

When *Mariner 9* slipped into orbit around Mars in 1971, it was the fourth NASA spacecraft to visit the planet. *Mariners 4, 6,* and *7* had made the trip from Earth several years before. These missions simply whisked past the planet, quickly taking some pictures and making some measurements. The pictures showed rough terrain pocked with *meteor craters* (holes left by falling meteors). None of the pictures from the flyby missions showed any signs of canals. But, because the pictures represented only a very small part of Mars's surface, the question of Martian canals was still open. It took *Mariner 9* to settle the question.

Mariner 9 arrived at Mars just when a planet-wide dust storm was raging. Nearly the entire surface of Mars

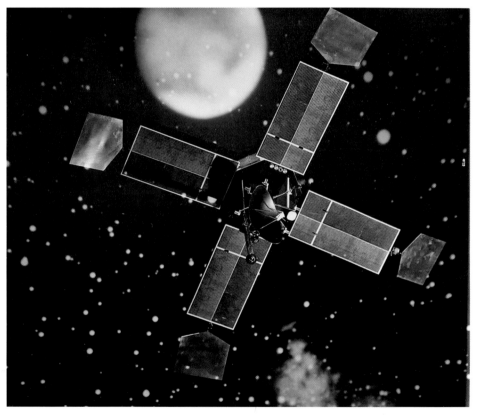

A model shows the *Mariner 4* spacecraft approaching Mars.

was blocked from view. But as the storm cleared, the spacecraft began to make major discoveries. Huge volcanic mountains began to poke out from the dusty clouds. Later, as more dust settled, a gigantic canyon could be seen.

During its mission, *Mariner 9* sent back 7,000 pictures of Mars. Altogether, the pictures covered 85 percent of its surface. In none of the pictures were there any signs of canals. What Schiaparelli and others had seen on Mars were shadows that seemed, in their imaginations, to form a network of canals.

Viking *Arrives*

Even before *Mariner 9* began sending back its pictures, another space mission to Mars was in the works. Because Mars has temperatures similar to those on Earth, an atmosphere, and small amounts of water, it was thought that Mars might also have living things on its surface. A new mission to Mars, *Viking,* was planned to look for signs of life. It would sample the planet's surface, measure surface weather, and take high-quality pictures. *Viking* consisted of four spacecraft. There were two orbiters that each carried a lander craft. After the orbiters went into orbit, they would begin taking pictures

NASA's *Viking* spacecraft consisted of an orbiter and a lander. Here, the lander is concealed in the rounded shell.

of Mars, and the landers would descend to the surface to conduct research there.

Viking 1 and *2* arrived in Mars orbit in 1976. They dropped their landers to the surface by parachutes and small rocket engines. Settling down on three legs, each lander extended a sample arm that scooped up soil for analysis.

The first close-up of the Martian surface was taken by the *Viking 1* lander on July 20, 1976. The metal saucer is one of the three lander footpads.

The Martian Surface

Pictures from the *Mariner* and *Viking* missions have revealed Mars to be an extraordinary world. It seems to be divided in half. The dividing line is marked in places by a cliff half a mile (nearly 1 kilometer) high. The cliff extends around Mars at an angle of 35 degrees to the

Martian equator. On the northern side of the cliff are lowlands that have few meteor craters. To the south is a rugged highland pocked with many craters.

Although the northern portion of Mars has few craters, the land is of great interest to scientists. It is marked with all sorts of surface *erosion* features made by wind and running water. In many places there are intricate networks of channels that had to be made by flowing

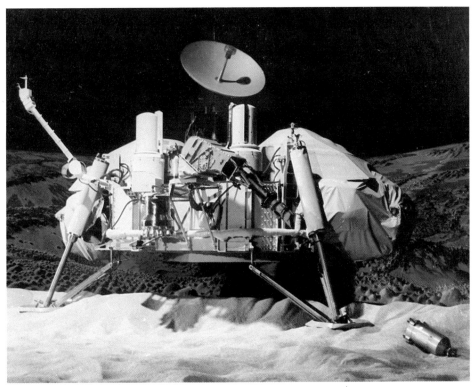

This painting shows the *Viking* lander as it appeared on Mars.

water. (These channels should not be confused with the *canali* that Schiaparelli thought he had seen on Mars. The real Martian channels are much too small to have been seen in Schiaparelli's telescope.) One of the big questions scientists have today is: Where is the water that made the channels?

The volcanoes of Mars are fantastic. There is nothing like them on Earth. Located just north of the equator is what geologists now call the Tharsis Region. It is a giant bulge in the surface of Mars that extends about 5,000 miles (8,000 kilometers) and reaches up to 4 miles

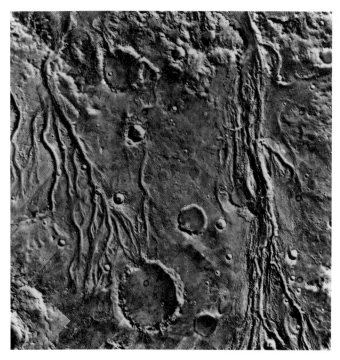

Small channels twist and braid across many areas of Mars. They may have been carved by water long ago.

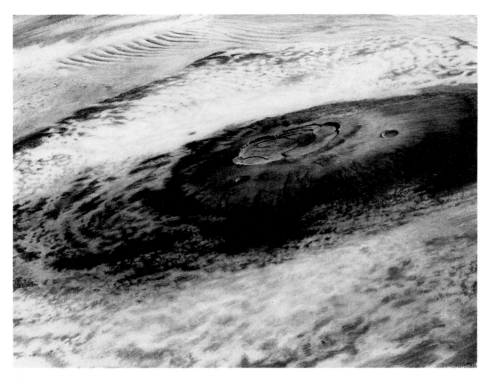

An artist's drawing of *Olympus Mons,* the largest Martian volcano.

(6.4 kilometers) high. Three enormous volcanoes, *Ascraeus Mons, Pavonis Mons,* and *Arsia Mons,* run in a line near the center of the ridge. Each is about 190 to 250 miles (300 to 400 kilometers) across and reaches up 17 miles (27 kilometers) above the surrounding Martian plain. Bigger still is a fourth volcano, *Olympus Mons.* Olympus Mons lies on the northwest flank of the ridge and is 435 miles (700 kilometers) across. It is three times taller than Mount Everest, the tallest mountain on Earth.

Valles Marineris, the Martian "Grand Canyon," stretches across the middle of the planet in this picture. Some of the Tharsis volcanoes are seen at left.

Each of these volcanoes has broad, sloping sides and is like the volcanoes that formed the Hawaiian Islands on Earth.

Still more fantastic than the volcanoes of Mars is the *Valles Marineris,* known as the Martian "Grand Can-

The huge impact crater in the center of this picture was named for the Italian astronomer Giovanni Schiaparelli, who thought he had discovered *canali,* or channels, on Mars.

yon." Beginning along the eastern edge of the Tharsis Region, it is a series of interconnecting canyons that stretch 3,100 miles (5,000 kilometers) from end to end. If the canyons could be brought to Earth, they would stretch completely across the United States. In places, the can-

This *Viking 2* picture shows a thin coating of frost on the reddish rocks and soil of Mars.

yons are more than 400 miles (650 kilometers) across and 23,000 feet (7,000 meters) deep.

Like Earth, Mars also has polar ice caps. The polar regions are partly like layer cakes made up of horizontal layers of dust and ice. The layers may mean that Mars has had periodic changes in its climate like the coming and going of the ice ages on Earth.

The Question of Life

One of the primary goals of the *Viking* landers was to search for signs of life. Each lander had a camera system that could spot plants such as small shrubs or moss. All the cameras saw was rock and sand-strewn plains.

Upon radio command from Earth, each lander extended a robot arm with a sample scoop at its end. Soil and small rocks were scooped up and dumped into funnels. The samples were then sent to miniature science laboratories inside the landers, where chemical tests were performed on them. If there were microscopic life in the soil of Mars, it was hoped that the tests would find it.

The *Viking 1* soil sampler scooped up samples of the Martian surface.

The test results were mixed. In other words, there might be life, or there might not be. Many scientists now think there isn't life on Mars, but no one knows for sure.

Exploring Mars: The Next Phase

Since the *Viking* spacecraft arrived at Mars, scientists have been studying the pictures and scientific data they sent back. Much is left to be learned.

Scientists hoped that a spacecraft called *Mars Observer* would provide new information about the Red Planet and answer some important questions, such as why the planet appears to be divided in half. The *Mars Observer* was scheduled to begin orbiting Mars in August 1993. It was equipped with more advanced cameras than the *Viking* orbiters. It also carried equipment to measure Mars's temperature, study its atmosphere, identify chemical elements on the surface, and search for a magnetic field.

The *Mars Observer* was to map Mars and its atmosphere for one complete orbit of the sun. Unfortunately, just as the *Mars Observer* was set to begin orbiting Mars, the spacecraft stopped transmitting radio signals. Scientists at NASA had no way of knowing what went wrong or whether the craft was in orbit. But it clearly was not able to send data back to Earth.

The ill-fated *Mars Observer* orbits Mars in this artist's drawing.

Other Mars missions were in the works, however. A Russian/European spacecraft, *Mars 94,* was to arrive in 1994 and drop two small landers and two surface penetrators, which would strike the surface and push into the soil to test its strength. Another Russian/European spacecraft was scheduled to arrive two years later. The *Mars 96* mission was to carry a landing craft that could move about the surface. It would also release a balloon that would float around in the thin Martian atmosphere, carrying scientific instruments. Since plans called for the *Mars Observer* to help relay scientific data collected by the surface craft from both these missions, scientists began searching for another way to fill this role.

Perhaps people will one day visit Mars to explore its mysteries. This is an artist's view of a mission to the *Valles Marineris*.

NASA is also planning future Mars missions. The Mars Environmental Survey Pathfinder Mission (MESUR Pathfinder) will send a variety of science instruments and roving vehicles to the Martian surface. MESUR Pathfinder may even collect some samples that will be rocketed back to Earth.

These missions to Mars may lead to an even greater adventure. Mars is perfect for human exploration because it is fairly close to Earth and livable, with proper protection. NASA and the space agencies of other nations are already planning for the day when the first human beings will set foot on Mars.

MARS QUICK FACTS

Mars: Named after the ancient Roman god of war.

	Mars	Earth
Average Distance from the Sun		
Millions of miles	142	93
Millions of kilometers	228	149.6
Revolution (one orbit around the sun)	1.88 Earth years	1 year
Average Orbital Speed		
Miles per second	15	18.6
Kilometers per second	24	30
Rotation (spinning once)	24 hours, 37 minutes	24 hours
Diameter at Equator		
Miles	4,222	7,926
Kilometers	6,794	12,756
Surface Gravity (compared with Earth's)	0.38	1
Mass (the amount of matter contained in Mars, compared with Earth)	0.11	1
Atmosphere	carbon dioxide, nitrogen, oxygen, water vapor	nitrogen, oxygen
Satellites (moons)	2	1

Mars's Moons	*Diameter**	*Distance From Planet*
Phobos	16 mi	5,829 mi
	25.7 km	9,380 km
Deimos	9.3 mi	14,590 mi
	15 km	23,480 km

*Mars's moons aren't round. The largest dimension is given.

GLOSSARY

Arsia Mons	A Martian volcano.
Ascraeus Mons	A Martian volcano.
Asteroids	Chunks of rock up to hundreds of miles across that orbit the sun.
Astronomer	A scientist who studies planets, moons, stars, and other objects in outer space.
Canali	The word given to the straight and curved lines that Giovanni Schiaparelli thought he saw on Mars.
Equator	An imaginary line around the middle of a planet and halfway between the planet's north and south poles.
Erosion	Wearing away of land surface by the forces of flowing wind, water, and ice.
Gravity	A force that causes objects to attract each other.
Mariner 4, 6, 7	NASA spacecraft that took pictures and measurements as they flew past the planet Mars.
Mariner 9	NASA spacecraft that orbited Mars in 1971 and took thousands of pictures of the Martian surface.
Mars 94, 96	Russian/European space missions to Mars that will deploy landers, penetrators, and balloons.
Mars Observer	NASA spacecraft that was to orbit Mars and map its surface.
MESUR	NASA Martian exploration program (Mars Environmental Survey Pathfinder Mission).
Meteor crater	A hole blasted out of the surface of a planet or moon by the impact of a meteor.
Olympus Mons	The largest Martian volcano.
Orbit	The path a planet takes to travel around the sun, or a moon to travel around a planet. (Also applies to the path a spacecraft follows when orbiting a planet or the sun.)

Pavonis Mons	A Martian volcano.
Penetrator	A scientific instrument that penetrates the ground to measure soil and rock beneath the surface.
Revolution	One complete orbit of a planet around the sun, or a moon around a planet.
Rotation	The spinning of a planet or moon around its axis.
Valles Marineris	The Martian "Grand Canyon."

FOR FURTHER READING

Asimov, I. *Isaac Asimov's Library of the Universe. Mars: Our Mysterious Neighbor.* Milwaukee, Wis.: Gareth Stevens Publishing, 1988.

Brewer, D. *Planet Guides: Mars.* New York: Marshall Cavendish, 1992.

Davis, D., and Cattermole, P. *Planetary Exploration: Mars.* New York: Facts on File, 1989.

Landau, E. *Mars.* New York: Franklin Watts, 1991.

NASA. *Mars: The Viking Discoveries,* NASA EP-146. Washington, D.C.: U.S. Government Printing Office, 1977.

NASA. *Our Solar System—A Geologic Snapshot,* NP 157. Washington, D.C.: National Aeronautics and Space Administration, 1991.

NASA. *Viking: The Exploration of Mars,* NASA EP-208. Washington, D.C.: U.S. Government Printing Office, 1984.

Vogt, G. *Viking and the Mars Landing: Missions in Space.* Brookfield, Conn.: The Millbrook Press, 1991.

INDEX

ABOUT THE AUTHOR

Gregory L. Vogt works for NASA's Education Division at the Johnson Space Center in Houston, Texas. He works with astronauts in developing educational videos for schools.

Mr. Vogt previously served as executive director of the Discovery World Museum of Science, Economics, and Technology in Milwaukee, Wisconsin, and as an eighth-grade science teacher. He holds bachelor's and master's degrees in science from the University of Wisconsin at Milwaukee, as well as a doctorate in curriculum and instruction from Oklahoma State University.